8/9/96

To John
for his kindness,
his sense of
mercy, and
his fine art.

My best wishes,
Natalie Kenvin

BOA
EDITIONS
LIMITED

BRUISE THEORY

Poems
by
Natalie Kenvin

Foreword by Carolyn Forché

BOA Editions, Ltd. ❧ Brockport, NY ❧ 1995

LC #: 95–75046
ISBN: 1–880238–20–9 cloth
ISBN: 1–880238–21–7 paper

First Edition
95 96 97 98   7 6 5 4 3 2 1

The publication of books by BOA Editions, Ltd.,
is made possible with the assistance of grants from
the Literature Program of the New York State Council on the Arts
and the Literature Program of the National Endowment for the Arts,
as well as from the Lannan Foundation, the Lila Wallace–Reader's Digest
Literary Publishers Marketing Development Program,
the Rochester Area Foundation, the County of Monroe, NY, and
contributions by individual supporters.

Cover Art: Edvard Munch, "Puberty" (1914), Munch Museum, Oslo
Photo: Munch Museum
Cover Design: Daphne Poulin
Typesetting: Richard Foerster
Manufacturing: McNaughton & Gunn, Lithographers
BOA Logo: Mirko

BOA Editions, Ltd.
A. Poulin, Jr., President
92 Park Avenue
Brockport, NY 14420

For Adrienne Smith (1934–1992), Joan Raisner,
Harvey Plotnick, and my children, Silvia and Paolo

CONTENTS

FOREWORD

*B*ruise Theory breaks the twenty-five year silence of poet Natalie Kenvin, imposed by poverty and isolation, fated as she was to have been born to struggling and harsh parents, to have suffered them and have plunged into a clinical depression that left her institutionalized and alone, relieved only by periods of respite in a world that offered little solace—that of a postwar American slum. If truth, as Walter Benjamin writes, "wants to be startled abruptly, at one stroke from her self-immersion, whether by uproar, music or cries of help," then truth has been startled by Kenvin's poems, as uproar, music, or a cry of help.

In 1960, when she was young and wandering the stacks of a library, Kenvin came upon the writings of a student of Freud, Marguerite Sechehaye, who had traced the descent into illness in *Reality Lost and Regained: Autobiography of a Schizophrenic Girl, With Analytic Interpretation,* and whose subject, herself impoverished, emerged whole through an act of sheer volition, through reclamation of language, itself resistant to pain. For twenty-five years, Kenvin held to the possibility of Sechehaye's triumphant restoration of selfhood. She read Gerard de Nerval's disturbing articulations of paranoia, and began to gather about her the works of other poets and writers who found the means to write their way through the labyrinthian passages of ecstatic and elevated states, metanoia, and illness. Meanwhile, she struggled to survive, working several jobs at once, and as a white woman, found comfort in an extended family of urban African-Americans.

Eventually she found full-time work, and with this measure of relief, began writing poems of raw power: fierce, compressed, and erotic. In them we hear the music of Dickinson and Plath, and experience a *frisson* familiar to their readers. In her *bone-orchard,* and through an *ephemeral meringue of fog,* along the *viper's track* of addiction, *in the clotheswhip/ air of March,* and *from the dark piece-eatings of butchery,* she records, as Kafka instructed, what she *sees among the ruins,* for she *sees different (and more) things than do the others.* The bruises examined in this book are actual, and they are also the marks of extremity, present as the evidence of what occurred. These poems are not *about* abuse, confinement, isolation, urban anonymity or sex. They offer us, in evidentiary language, poetic lucidity and strength, a glimpse of the mind at labor in the unknown.

—Carolyn Forché
March 1995

BRUISE THEORY

*Anyone who cannot come to terms with his life while he
is alive needs one hand to ward off a little his despair
over his fate . . . but with his other hand he can note
down what he sees among the ruins, for he sees different
(and more) things than do the others; after all, dead as
he is in his own life time, he is the real survivor.*

—Franz Kafka, Diary entry of October 19, 1921

BRUISE THEORY

Assume the day
Gives you no visible marks.

In sleep
Your desires derby-race
To a pit
Where bruises gather
In oil slicks.

Immigrant bruises
With stumbling speech,
Refugees who travel
On the decks of decaying ships.
Some have family names,
Some no names at all.

Sweetladymidnight bruises,
Perfumed knocks,
Blows, insults,
Curses of substance.

A host of bruises
In lumpy clothes,
A militia.

Massive, fernlike bruises
Delicate
As an afternoon insult.

Suppose one pummels its way out
Tonight.
Did it begin
The day your father
Cursed you?

The time your mother
Stood at the sink
And cried from a slap,
The smell of bleach,
Lemons, and vanilla
Lost in the clotheswhip air
Of March?

In sleep, the bruises
Bicker and shuffle,
An uprising of old plums.

❧

THE BLACK EYE

Your fist beat a knot on my face,
Polyphonous, clothed, densely erudite.
The winter was a lovely white.
All gypsy plaques and dewlaps
Could not undo this knobbed insult,
Relentless, misfractured, not painted.
Mazurkas, fandangos, jigs, abrupt
Blisters of music
Did not dampen or soothe
This ripely dark, evasive, shadowed bruise
Growing as a bone-orchard savors decay.
The ephemeral meringue of fog
Rose in a poverty of oxygen,
A mishap of touch.
My eye, mashed blue, adroop in fading light.
The winter was a lovely white.

PROM NIGHT AT GROSSE POINTE HIGH
AND LAFAYETTE CLINIC

The boys wear tuxedos
That hang in great, dark wardrobes.
The girls are pink and silver,
Their impassive throats adorned
With lace.
They live soldered to their mothers.
The pearl pins in their corsages
Clip roses, carnations to their breasts,
Pitifully sweet.
But I am standing in the laundry room
At the back of a ward of beds.
My pinstripe robe is stamped with my name.
Denny, the night aide, pours wine
Into a paper cup half filled with Kool Aid.
My nipple stiffens under touch,
Erect as a meringue.
His stubby black fingers close
Around my arm.
"You're a sweet girl," he says.

THE BAD MOTHER

Drinking peach wine,
The bad mother is strong.
She carries an iron box
With a stubby key
And horrible letters inside.
Roused, she moves
Slowly, sluggish
But elusive.
Her glebe tit hangs snub
In a pink bra,
Her hair secured with
A hairpin of fear.
A man cursed her once,
So she melted his spine
To a drop of wax.
Her eye is a sinister violet.
She sighs.
A coffin splits deep in a grave.

LOVE POEM TO STEVEN

*Recovery from heroin addiction involves 3 to 5
percent of active users.*
            —The Psychology of Addiction

I

Rust on the razor
That threatens the throat,
Would I have loved you
Without the viper's track
That marks your arm?
No.
That scratch-tongued wager
Was a part of us.
The viper's tongue-harp
Does not sing.
It is silent as dust.
Your genitals hang slack
Inside the gloom of a pantsleg.
The smell of hashbrowns
And boiled coffee
Is cut with bacon grease.
The morning congeals.
A tan fur-patched mongrel
Lopes through the alley
Nosing scraps,
Lapping flat pools of spill.

II

Will I sleep again
Key taped to my leg?
No.
These times are gone.
Do you live again
To be beaten until
No one recognizes your face?
Only the stray hairs
Of these ghost hags remain.
They are gone.

III

Your mouth tastes bitter as a dandelion.
We lie in the sun,
A self-figured knot
And snarl.
Glut like a sack,
I sleep inside your shirt.
Where is the silence that condemns,
The evening that bruises?
It's a time of scraps,
Cold bonds.

SKIN HUNGER

You hold me like you'd clutch
The tough, slippery chassis
Of a mannequin
You really loved.
We lie in a practical ache.
My mouth opens, avid for sweets.
My bones loosen.
The music I hear is cuntmusic,
The womb's velvety longing,
Empty women keening hard
For something lost.
It is a want no bone can hold,
No thrum or probe can stop.
It is a blank unspoken murder
Like a pulled tooth,
A wineshop, a tavern
Of odors. From this clump
The white and purple scents of mucus
Mix and rise.
We lie in the simmering confusion
Of wasps.

LET MY MOUTH TAKE YOU

Resilient and coarse as a marigold,
This cock
Will fit
Inside my cold lip,
Edible, stiff and saliva-sleek.
Dark juices will begin to flood
The blue cave of my mouth
With a bitter, thick liquid.
I choke, sweat,
Begin to cry.
Semen glides past my lips
In a silky clump,
Oozes sullen down my throat
With the taste of bile and thyme.
I swallow your shapeless, meandering
Existence whole
Like a gulp of velveteen.

FOR SILVIA, MY DAUGHTER, CHICAGO READ MENTAL HEALTH CENTER, SUMMER 1988

There is a plain cruelty of light
Where ghosts are dense,
Lovely ethers that float in the air.
It is here in the fields that surround
The institution that I recall you,
Here in summer with the smell of scorched hay,
Grass and chamomile flowers.
Mother, do you remember me
Before I was sick?
The sticky crumb
Becomes a cinder
Burnt to darkness.
I do remember you.
We are apart now, severed
As decay severs the living
From the dead
In leaves and flowers.
Your smile is faint
As I move the brush. I braid
Your blonde hair between my thumb
And forefinger.
Contentment is a pharmacy of sweets
Narrowing to the pain
In the stripe of a wildflower.
A black-haired woman with a bulky cardigan
And no socks
Pulls my daughter's sleeve.
"Give me fifty cents.
Give me a piece of that candy."
"I don't have any money.
Get away from me," says my daughter
In a voice clear as water.

She stands still in the large dayroom
Of the ward.
In the sunlight,
Her grief has turned hard as amber.

SOME OF THE THINGS I SEE FOR YOU

For my daughter

You will be famous, your mouth
Staunched with a marigold.
You will be remembered like
The ache of a kicked shin,
Or a bruise rising under the skin.
You will sustain
The perilous loneliness of a profile.
Knuckle, throat and eye
Will be flesh remembered solemn,
Black as the sulk of basalt.
You will be the blood of red trillium
And false mermaid spilled in spring.
You will be the long tongues of moths
That drink from swamp orchids.
You will be stillness,
A whipstalk of grace,
The cruel gaze of silk,
The hot wink
Of a black-eyed pea,
The dumb, ponderous softness
Of a guava,
The grace of a mare.
Gluttonous, solitary larva,
You will eat the world.

MY DAUGHTER IS ILL IN SPRING
AND SUMMER

Things have a lack of season
And seasoning
With you so gone into darkness.
No pepper-spice of incident
No licorice tinge of after
No fortune's habitat or
Ouija board simple
Outcome.
The bells are like pilgrims
With their travelling-Jesus tongues
Ripped from their mouths.
The red dahlia's spears thrust from
The yellow craw at its center.
I turn to Venus of the
Deceptive flap,
The listening wall:
She has the wisdom
Of smoke
Or a straight-rising prayer
Of steam.
She governs the pull
Of dilating moons.
We drink the broth of dreams.
The poppy and bluestem daisy
Hang sullen orange and white;
Free from the dark piece-eatings
Of butchery
In the drowse of night.

MY DAUGHTER

My daughter is a fantail carp
Dissolving to the glass fisheye
Of the sun.
She is the sheep's cold blooming
Melting to cotton, wool,
The stunned captain of no ship.
She is a white butterfly beating ragged
In the nappyheaded moon,
A wise outcast,
Dumb, freed and wingbruised real.
In darkness she turns.

HEAVY DAUGHTER BLUES

I love her for the same reason
The poor love sweets,
Or Black kids play boom boxes
Hard in the anger of I am.
In wintersour light,
My daughter ties me up.
White woman, prepare to die.
She is the red, the bronze, the
Black,
All that is lost she will get back.
But it is too late,
She is old enough
To leave.
She plays too rough for me.
Bring me juju bones of spoken form.
Bring a blue stalk from the butcher's
Heart.
She sits on my neck.
My death will be insignificant,
A disgrace.
Better for me to drink
From the large pain that lets us
Sink,
Become the river itself.
She is heavy in her grief.

MY DAUGHTER IS SLEEPING

My daughter is sleeping
On the floor next to me.
The room is small:
Two mattresses, dishevelled clothes,
An empty glass, a cat,
The smell of veal and almonds.
Night and the shrivelled rouge
Of a geranium.
Her body lies in a peel
Of skin.
Her neck is like the stem
Of a chrysanthemum,
Supple, brown, dead.
It twists in ease,
Torpor leadlaced in hair and air and eye.
There is bitterness
In the mummied wings of her shoulder blades.
The dreamer is reversed in blackness,
In the lecherous deletions of sleep.

MY DAUGHTER'S MATTRESS

My daughter disappeared three years ago. She has been in hospitals ever since. She tells me: "Don't throw out my mattress. I will need it." For the first seven months she was gone, I made her bed. Then I hauled the mattress downstairs to the basement, its grey tufts heaving. Later I dragged it back upstairs and moved it to the kitchen. Now it rests on end against the far wall, next to a shelf with cans of pinto beans and peas, under a sheet lightly coated with black cat hair. Small clusters of blue flowers stand out on it. They turn the mattress and air the house when someone dies. On the ceiling there is a bare kitchen bulb suspended by a brown, oily strand of cord. On the street outside, traffic is brisk. In our intimacy with alleys, we dream of serious love and bad luck. In the apartment, I clean, place pairs of shoes in lines, shake out the scrap rugs on the floor. I keep putting things away.

CHILD SUPPER

To my daughter, who cannot live in the world.

I

I am packing your things again.
I wrap a glass reindeer. It stands
Stiff-legged, staring forward,
A smaller reindeer caught in its belly.
The spaces between us are solid,
Taffeta-black.
The defrosting refrigerator smells
Of the small death of ice.
I look at paintings, drawings, postcards
From friends.
This is my child supper.
I eat with violent candor.

II

But you will come back.
It's an old story this one,
An old lie;
I will tell it
Until you die
Or until you satisfy
Some man's dull vegetable brutality.

III

Daughter's reply: Four years in hospitals,
I know the solitary power
Of a long illness,
Have the peculiar, peevish wishes
Of the sick.
You are cold, distant,
The nurse of no one.
Only say that you love me
And I will not walk
The long, sad parallels
Of those who wait for nothing.
I live like a cellar animal,
A vole, or termite,
Voyeur of the wainscot.
But you do not answer.
High in the stubborn twilight
I want to eat black ash burning wild.
I think I will die
In some war to rid the world of pain.
I have never been your child.

NUPTIAL SUBSTANCE

A bud, without a doubt,
Turns out to be sweet and grows rotten.
April under your heel
Wields plain-spoken trouble.
If Moses is a rover, I want his journey.
Her hair smelled like cinnamon,
Her knuckles slick with bleach.
The folds outside her womb
Are white slits cleft blue,
Violet with witch shadows.
The smells of come and anise
      mix in the air.
She takes me like a bear
      eats honey,
Her soft fur soaked in
      numb sleep.
We are flooded with poppies.

EXPULSION

The brief upholstery of bone and muscle
Nipped and annihilated,
These clumps
Float down drains, conduits.
Blood turns to water,
To nothing, absolved.
Even if I had a son
Who was a giant,
I would not forget
These small dealings of bone,
For in each ripe cluster and globule
Lie the sprout and pouch of a man.
Each is a swarm,
A disorder of dead proportion.
Here are nipples and eyelashes,
The earliest stuff
Of dream and memory,
Each alone in its dark tent.

DINER

The men smell
Of petroleum
And overwork,
The stink of
Cigarettes and
A swine smell
Marinated with
Dust on skin,
Paint in hair.
It is noon.
The newspapers
They hold
Are full of murders
And big smiles.
One sits at the counter
As though straddling
A mare.
The taste of my saliva
Is thin and bitter
Like smoke.
Their talk has a
Common malignancy
Like a growth of gum
Stuck under a chair.
A siren skins
The afternoon.

KIWI

The stubby brown fur of your outside
Is rough, hobgoblin suede.
Your black seeds grow large, click
Like billiard balls or comets
Crashing out of orbit around a green sun
In the slick doubt of space.
In green, divided light,
Spokes and rays emanate from a pale center.
You are a slippery coagulate,
A cathedral filled with the warm, dumb
Succulence of fruit, a planet.

MEAT AND MEMORY

When my father receded, I became small
Like a stain, an apostrophe of blood.
Now I long to be darkly full.
I want to get back to his marrow and root.
In the market I stare at packets of meat,
Blood loose beneath the cellophane,
Sap from a sticky wound.
Portions are mapped on the side of a cow
As though they were countries,
The ruby geography of grist and bone.
I miss him,
But all is altered inside.
I hear my death in the drying of blood,
The smell of meat and memory.

THE BAD BUILDING

Two blocks from John Your Friend from Pakistan's Bar and the Nubian Lady Hair Salon is the Bad Building. It is two blocks off Clark Street, just past the alley. In the alley are mattresses, bags of garbage with the blood of chickens, white plastic forks, rinds of sandilla, mashed beet, blackened banana, discarded filet. The building is half a block long. In front of it is a bald rise of dirt that might have been a lawn. Empty cans of Tecate and Schlitz, a dirty Pamper, a Snickers wrapper, sticks from *paletas*, covered with syrup, lie on the ground. Everybody in my neighborhood knows the bad building.

A sign in the entranceway says the exterminator is coming on Wednesday *"por los ratos y ratones."* A balada moans, *"Y tu sabes que senti,"* drifting on the summer air. The children on the steps have sweet popsicle juice smeared around their mouths. They twist left and right. Their spindly legs have maps of dirt on them.

The men lie on the ground or slouch near the old cars parked in front of the bad building. Their nails are grey with grease. They work endlessly on the dumb, stalled machines, deftly fingering their inner parts, talking in flourishes, sipping beer. The smells of grease and smoke, diapers, boiled beans, urine and potato peels hang in the air mixed with love songs.

The mothers move like heifers. They smell of baby powder and menstrual blood. Barrettes hold the older girls' dark hair in slick clumps. They wear canvas shoes and smell of carnation spice and meanness.

The moon rises dead like the smell of a dime held in a fist.

The ripe stink of brilliantine,
Close bristle and hot breath
Comes from the group,
Slack-jacketed in slick-ass jeans
In the park.
They box, bunch, gab,
Show their colors.
They stand in twilight,
Their shadows sinuous, nagging.
They sniff at the bitter dark.
PVR. Eduardo, Tony, Bob.
Sudden blood.
I know them,
Misery in a pantsleg,
Grope and be gone.
They have the unkillable smell
Of puberty: Leather, clove,
And the pitting fault of sweat.
Later Tony will
Pump some skinny white chick.
Bob will let a black whore
Gulp him like an aspirin.
These three tight belts
Lurk heavy,
The dark hollow of their cheeks
Nibbled clean with waiting.

DEMETER

The first thing you know
She's lost,
A runaway with a dark man
And an attitude.
I look in every Greyhound station
Filled with the blue and silver paranoia
Of small town lives.

She's missing,
Her finger on the amber lip
Of a beer bottle,
Its sour malt confused
With the smell of my thighs.
Have you seen her?
My friends say I'm too good to my children,
Too hard on myself.

Every six months I look for her
While she moves in the tactless hallways
Of hard sleep.
Somewhere she eats cold chili
In a flimsy slip,
Ignoring the dreams of wallpaper.

THE DREAM OF SOMETHING PERFECT

My moor, my Egyptian,
My familiar, dense particular.
See the soft fire
In the blossoms of foxglove,
Pockets of shadow
In a dark house.
The crevasse in a bobby pin,
The quick iridescence of a bruise,
A taut, lumpy collision
On cauliflower skin.
When the night air
Is full of noises,
I dream of something perfect,
Zero, no
In some fine calculation
Of dust and gypsum,
Resistant as the white
Of the open mind
Or the blue acetylene sputter
Of a cornflower.
The body disappears
Singing history
On the air of winter.
White bones click, pop.
We have no secrets
Except the tendon of the foot
In first light.
We hope to put down
The fierceness of a root.
We taste salt and drink
The bitter nitrates
Of chemistry.

A gash, a slit,
Shut close and sleeping
Like halves of an avocado
For a most immediate knife.
It is a thick mud nest
Of twigs, a hair pie
Marked by the toes of starlings.
If its fleshy lip
Could sing or squeak
Like mink or polished wood,
It would sing sharp
Above skin of spookhouse vanilla.
In the stink and roam of her,
Lady mudflap pouts.
She is a moist rumor,
Secret like blood
Held under the tongue.
She is a nest of weeds
Replete with seeds.

TO A PENIS

Let us ignore the government suspicion
     of the weirdly stiff and dour.
Let us ignore the dry revival
     of the worm's sexless anarchy.
Love dwindles to a flaccid stump,
     dumb, flabby, lightweight
In shapeless timidity.
Pygmy beautiful grower,
Your insolent logic
Can be a horror,
Hiding in swapped genitals.
A sour flavor surrounds your thirst,
Oozes through your root
Drinking itself cool
In a cloud of sperm,
     a crust, a cold dream of frost.
My rough wife,
You bury yourself direct
     in profound abundance.

TATTOOS

Floating carp,
Rampant dragons, tigers that ripple
With a flick of skin.
They are like stencils of milk
On burlap.
They lash their tails
In the brightness of pain.
Insolent stencils that pin memory
To a tree, a rose.
Soaked, caustic wires, they hum blue
Above minute streams of blood.
They are the curves
Where dreams grieve and tilt
Up to light.
Headstones on skin,
They are hard appetites
Of bitterness.

FARTS

Presumptuous, misbehaved stigmas,
They flare;
Breaking the rules of strict camouflage,
They hover askew in air
Like the wings of hunchbacked angels.
These worldly vapors,
Sour pearls,
Dainty shadows, these intercessions
Fend off new air
Like a purple garment,
Extravagant, pressed.
They are softly compassionate,
Unspoken stresses
That float on the air, heavy
Like the scent of magnolia.
From their soft velvet stink
Comes a gaunt nimbus
Of blue flame.

Time is a visible lie
Like the black roots of blonde hair.
Women,
Punching bags,
Old bags.
Cubans seep their slick roots
In blondes who have a way
With whitemen.
Everything is all
Tough go and putback,
No costume.
And me, the outboy,
The common woman,
Tidy as the life of a crease.
Thorns, ice, soot, nipples,
Hair, a cut knee.
A raw dog,
A Thursday tooth,
A porcelain chip of spine.
She'll swallow an egg whole,
Common as a moan.

THE CURSE

What does it take
To love a stain
So incomplete
It slips like a pirate
Through the temperamental
Hair of the pubis,
Political, wise, sedate?
Thing of unknown and forbidden taste.
What is its taste?
Dark, coating the tongue,
Sour as semen
Or airy as thyme.
A chemistry of strange sugars
Produces this sticky rapture,
These gouts with a gallish smell
Of death,
A heavy weight,
Sluggish, elusive.
Simple as spittle,
These streams each woman makes
Are the stems of flowers that become
An immense Peruvian river,
Dark as a wineclot.

THE ICE KING SLEEPS WITH HIS BRIDE

They lie in an embrace,
In a sharp bolt of spent cold.
He lives in air.
She breathes alone
Beneath moistened bones
Under the dark down of a wing.
They lie in the perverse
Chemistry of skin.
Winter's icy cock
Hangs sweet as a billy club
In this white place
Where nothing cries.
Some nameless power
Has made a pact,
A buckshot curse
That will contract
The world in pain.

INSOMNIA

Gluttonous, solitary larva,
You weave a loophole of days.
You hide in the three-fingered gloves
Of gentlemen,
In the sad, pocked rise of yeast
And the mushroom oozing dew.
You become the white garrote of solitude.
A labyrinth of uncertainty
Marks your growing place.

THE OLD QUEEN LOOKS AT WINTER

After Gerard de Nerval

The king, the old pervert, is dying.
He was lord of volcanoes, king of winter.
His beard's plutonic bristles
Hid the dark arch of his jaw.
Bind his crook feet,
Blind his cross eye!

Fruit hangs in the orchard.
In ruins of twilight,
I once sought the garden's fountain,
But found only a grey devil
Howling in a stoup of holy water.

Still the bonelust strives and courts
A mildewed purse of chicken hearts,
A sagging glove
This drupe, my womb, will save.

January loses her chemise,
July its slipper
In the chill yearfeast.

PLAYING PINOCHLE AT LAFAYETTE CLINIC

I

In the distinct, harsh days
Of November, I ran away.
At seventeen I traveled small.
My blue poplin windbreaker had a hole
In the left pocket.
I fell asleep in someone's garage
Before they found me,
The dead, bitter taste of barbiturates
On my tongue.

II

Four of us sit at a small wooden table
On the ward: Gary, Denny, the nurse's aide,
Reba and me.
Gary, the Royal Oak sniper, taught me
How to play pinochle. He hid in a tree and shot
Two women in the back. His large curly head
Moves to one side.
If he stays here long enough,
He won't have to go to prison.
He and I are the old-timers.

III

Reba stands at the closed window.
It is an early spring night.
There is the snap and ache of ice
When it is chill,
Turning into water.

IV

Denny sits across from me,
His head shining like an oiled plum.
The cards pop and click as he whips them down,
Rakes in a trick with his left hand.
"Shee it," he says.
Reba sits next to him,
Sixteen, another runaway,
Dyed blonde hair bevelled around her face.
Denny is hopelessly in love.
He crushes the shell of a peppermint in his teeth,
Watches the slide of thigh as her legs cross.
He brings her candy bars of milk chocolate
And gooey caramel; even a pack of cards
With the fragrance of new paper and luck.

V

Reba sits still, her face upturned,
Sweet, insolent,
A blank delinquent
No one can flatter.

VI

Last night I danced wildly,
Holding a patient's pair of long johns
I had taken to repair
At arm's length,
Seat flapping open,
My odd partner.

VII

Tonight Reba, Gary, and I wait at the table
For evening to fall.
Who will flatter us
With stories of births and barbecues?
We have no visitors.
Time is suspended
Like an unpleasant holiday.

VIII

We sit late, we four.
The game is long.
When we rise, we each inhale
An exhausted rush of tiredness,
The longing for sleep.

IX

I go to my room.
The sway and soothe of dark
Picks me up, closes over me,
Smells my heady animal smell,
Laps me in a confused sleep
Tasting of vanilla, burnt sugar, valium.

X

Smooth sister, I look for you
In an hour of linear angel dust
And the lamps of halogen magi.
You are my deep sweet,
My drowsy bonbon,
My root exotic.
On the ward
There is a congress of small breaths
From open mouths.
Here are the exulting, monstrous translations
Of the night.

ELIZABETH WALKS IN THE AIR
ABOVE PENNSYLVANIA

She is dreaming of the damp press
Of fox tracks,
The dumb, blunt decay of yam
Waxed fat.
The soles of her feet track silt.
She is a shape, a transport
Sag and sour.
In the tense ripple of wind
And the press of sleep,
She glides over marsh grass,
Over blast furnace, where heat blooms
Like an orange-grey lily.
She is invincible as yeast.
Her dark gnarled foot
Becomes a walking root.

EVANGELICAL DARK AND A MARSH

Swamp water is slow to turn.
The cattail sulks.
The white lily burns brown in mulch.
Darkness is numb and soothing like velvet.
Night has Marsh light,
Cold, glacial.
Night has the cool
Smell of decay and the color of lilacs.
Brown spores fleck the underside of
Staghorn ferns.
A cricket carries the dark
On her back.
Gold flecks of algae move slowly in brackish water
Like the eyes of peacocks.

SEIZURE RHAPSODY

I

A seizure is the body's tantrum,
A going down into darkness, to nothing,
A coming of memory and muscle.
The seizure itself is desire,
Relief from the self,
The prisoner let out
In a catechism of starts.

II

My mother
          doesn't remember
          what first
          happened to me,
recalls nothing.
Except that,
          when I was small,
My father
          came home drunk,
          wanted to pick me up.
I slipped
          from her arms,
My head split open
I fell
          or was I thrown?

III

After each black tantrum,
Fatigue, sleep...
I dream of vultures
And the original kiss,
A damp betrayal by vowels.
I am a despicable starling
That cannot fly.
Here are aches and cinders,
Blood held
      on the tongue,
Hopeless milk inside the mouths
      of small children
Afraid to speak.
I live at the end of things
Where emptiness wheels
      dark and slow
Like the phosphorus zeroes
      of the air.

TO SUSAN WISHCOP, AN OJIBWA BURIED IN THE INDIAN CEMETERY PAST BEAVER BAY, COUNTY #4, MINNESOTA

Your mouth stings, full of pointy weeds.
The ground in this thicket
Is overgrown with wild quinine, white daisies,
And red clover. Your weed pasture.
Red pines creak in the wind.
Smell of hay and weedrot.
Fever killed you.
You died about the time
John Beargrease became known
For delivering mail to people on the North Shore
By dogsled. Milkweed pods split open
On the Temperance River.
The boards on your tarpaper shack
Turned ashy in the afternoon sun.
You lay in the dark with Anowah Wishcop, your husband,
Your skin bruised, dreaming of mint and wild roses.
You lie here with Aikian Beargrease, Joe Beargrease,
Joe Yellowbird, Mrs. Yellowbird.
You have the dust of the world
Under your nails.

BEATING

My father knows only that
There is a humid readiness
About my mother,
Her hair messy, lying in ringlets
That smell of copper.
Now she is going to get it,
He says.
He strikes her once and she falls
Back from the medicinal, calloused skid
Of his right hand.
Now he is balancing on top of
Her fallen body with his left leg,
His right suspended in the air
As one might balance on a log.
She says, "Don't."
For a moment they are caught here
In the spit of craziness.
He lets her up.
They walk to the kitchen.
They sit at the table
In a convalescent indolence,
A queer lassitude.
He pours a curl of cream into her tea,
Turning it a tarnished color.
She drinks, hooking her fingers
Around the cup.
He eats a small cracker.
I stare at them.
They are shameless
And in a great solitude.

PARADISE VALLEY, DETROIT

Sweetie holds a Kool in her right hand.
She sleeps sitting up in a chair
In the living room,
Five people and one bed in the house.
She puts cocoa butter on the pink scar
On Lana's forehead to make it fade,
Cuts her hair when the moon is waxing,
Saying this is the right time
To cut things.
Fingernails, loose quarters, slick
Chitterlings and Pitty-Pat.
Across the hall, Lana's play-mother
Wet-combs her hair. The room fills
With the smell of Dixie Peach and lye.
Billy B. says that women
Are lovely pink traps
And have strange, leaving ways.
He gets drunk on Thunderbird.
His eyes roll sloppy,
And he walks like a rooster,
Dipping and cursing,
His black suspenders stretching
Over a sluice of gut.
Sweetie's high cheekbones are indigo blue
In the glare of the television.
The whites of her eyes
Are like salt
Crusted on roses.

Heat sleeps inside the slow mattresses
Of the house
And in her carpet slippers
Lapping the floor.
She sits alone in the dark
With the puny voodoo stink
Of her cigarette.

SWEETIE AT LEICESTER COURT

I

Up Woodward on Leicester Court
Summer is cut open
Like a yam steaming in its jacket.
Police ride four in a car,
Skirting the edge of Paradise Valley.
Sweetie listens to laughter and sweet
Doo-wop fuck-yous from the street.
Here in the hallway is the smell of piss,
Mustard greens, fatback and pinto beans.
As I walk,
Voices drift from the windows:
"Hello white girl."

II

They released me from the state institution
In the fall.
I lived on my own until Sweetie took me in.
The faces of young men
Walking down Woodward
Are purple and grey, ghostly orchids
In twilight.
They like the city,
Walk its disordered backstep.

III

The gender of darkness is female,
Sweetly pubic, closing over itself
Like the halves of a prune.
It holds the sleeping bodies of
Butter-Upper, Sweetie's husband,
And Karlayne, her granddaughter.
In the big double bed, the calluses
On the bottom of their feet are dark maroon
And yellow, tough skin which slides against
The topsheet.
Maybe the dark is marcelled in great, stiff
Waves
Like Sweetie's hair.

IV

Sweetie tells us stories in Spanish,
Drives us to a Mexican restaurant at 3:00 a.m.,
The fins of her Pontiac moving slowly through
The night. We eat sweet cactus and drink cocoa,
Come home and fall asleep on the couch and the floor
By the T.V.
Sweetie sleeps upright in her armchair,
Wakes at seven to go to work,
Leaving us asleep.
She tells me: "You were never crazy, just
Too much alone."

SWEETIE ELIZABETH HOUSE AND HER FAMILY VISIT ME IN ANN ARBOR, MICHIGAN

I

Yellow peppers cooking in a cast-iron skillet
With gravy and pork chops.
Sweetie Elizabeth House, Betty Carole, Lana,
Grandmother, mother, granddaughter
Rolled together in the large double bed,
Mouths open in the dark,
The little corpses of empty shoes
Aligned on the floor.
We stand in the kitchen.
I laugh so hard I stagger
And put my hand on Sweetie's shoulder.
We talk about what colors become them:
Lana, fourteen, purplish-black like eggplant,
And Silvia, one.
Lana holds my daughter on her lap.
The curlicue of black braid
Touches the blonde crown of the baby's head.
The baby eats what molds, stinks, smells sweet.
We talk about how Nettie got so fat
And the fickleness of men.
The roots of Sweetie's hair are stiff
With pomade and the smoke of Kools.
Soon the three of them will drive away
In the big Pontiac, back to Detroit.

II

To Sweetie, who could never come inside
my real mother's house.

Close mother,
I remember you salt and sour
Like the seep of grease.
Missing you one place, I search another.
Somewhere I stop, waiting for you
Among the dark porches of grudging wood,
Among the dust sifting interminable, fine on front
       stoops,
Among the heaviness of minerals.
You are a sweet, ghostly narcotic,
A taste, a scrap, a bone to end things.
I look for you in the moonshine
Of white skin hoodoo,
Among the wisps of raffia that burn to nothing,
Hissing in the wind.

Acknowledgments

Grateful acknowledgment is made to the editors of the following journals where some of these poems first appeared:

Cats Eye: "The Dream of Something Perfect";

Columbia Poetry Review: "The Bad Mother," "Beating," "The Curse," "Cynthia Cinderella Columbus," "Love Poem to Steven," "My Daughter Is Sleeping," "Paradise Valley, Detroit," "Prom Night at Grosse Pointe High and Lafayette Clinic," and "Skin Hunger";

5 a.m.: "Heavy Daughter Blues;"

Hairtrigger: "Bruise Theory";

Hawaii Review: "My Daughter";

New American Writing: "Visible Lie";

No Roses Review: "Seizure Rhapsody";

Phoebe: "The Bad Building" and "Nuptial Substance";

Poetpourri: "The Black Eye" and "Tattoos";

Private: "To Susan Wishcop..." and "To a Penis";

So to Speak: "Child Supper";

Taos Review: "Sweetie Elizabeth House and Her Family Visit Me in Ann Arbor, Michigan";

Wyrd Women-Word Women: "Lady Mudflap."

The poem "Bruise Theory" took its title from Gail White's "Theory of the Bruises." The line "Suppose one pummels its way out tonight" was suggested by her phrase "Say one beats its way out tonight." The title of the poem "Meat and Memory" was borrowed from Deborah Pintonelli. The idea of the cartography of meat was suggested by Mary Hawley. The phrase "I hear my death in the drying of blood" from the same poem comes from Graham Lewis. In the poem "Beating," the phrases "convalescent indolence" and "queer lassitude" are taken from Alice Munro's short story "Royal Beating." The title "Heavy Daughter Blues" was taken from Wanda Coleman's book of the same name. The phrase "all kinds of hollow nobodies" was taken from William Straw. The images "intimacy with alleys" and "monstrous translations of the night" are from Gwendolyn Brooks. The line "I keep putting things away" was suggested by her poem "The Bean Eaters." The last two lines of "Lady Mudflap" were taken from a poem by Keith Waldrop. Finally, several images in "Kiwi" were suggested by poems of Pablo Neruda.

I want to acknowledge the help of my typist, Sharon Lenahan, as well as that of numerous other people. Without the guidance and encouragement of Paul Hoover and Carolyn Forché, my teachers, I would never have been able to produce *Bruise Theory*. I also wish to thank Elizabeth Blair, Juanita Garza, and Carolyn Koo for their comments regarding the manuscript. Finally, without the patience and devotion of my husband, Harvey Plotnick, I would never have been able to finish this book.

About the Author

A longtime Chicago resident, Natalie Kenvin teaches English as a Second Language, poetry, and creative writing at Wilbur Wright College. Her poetry has appeared in a number of journals, including *Columbia Poetry Review, Taos Review,* and *New American Writing.* She edits *No Roses Review* (with Jaunita Garza and Carolyn Koo), a magazine of poetry and short fiction. She has received awards from the Ragdale Foundation, the Illinois Arts Council, and Associated Writing Programs. She received a National Endowment for the Arts Grant in January 1995.

BOA EDITIONS, LTD.

NEW POETS OF AMERICA SERIES

Vol. 1   *Cedarhome*
          Poems by Barton Sutter
          Foreword by W.D. Snodgrass

Vol. 2   *Beast Is a Wolf with Brown Fire*
          Poems by Barry Wallenstein
          Foreword by M.L. Rosenthal

Vol. 3   *Along the Dark Shore*
          Poems by Edward Byrne
          Foreword by John Ashbery

Vol. 4   *Anchor Dragging*
          Poems by Anthony Piccione
          Foreword by Archibald MacLeish

Vol. 5   *Eggs in the Lake*
          Poems by Daniela Gioseffi
          Foreword by John Logan

Vol. 6   *Moving the House*
          Poems by Ingrid Wendt
          Foreword by William Stafford

Vol. 7   *Whomp and Moonshiver*
          Poems by Thomas Whitbread
          Foreword by Richard Wilbur

Vol. 8   *Where We Live*
          Poems by Peter Makuck
          Foreword by Louis Simpson

Vol. 9   *Rose*
          Poems by Li-Young Lee
          Foreword by Gerald Stern

Vol. 10   *Genesis*
          Poems by Emanuel di Pasquale
          Foreword by X.J. Kennedy

Vol. 11   *Borders*
          Poems by Mary Crow
          Foreword by David Ignatow

Vol. 12   *Awake*
          Poems by Dorianne Laux
          Foreword by Philip Levine

Vol. 13   *Hurricane Walk*
          Poems by Diann Blakely Shoaf
          Foreword by William Matthews

Vol. 14   *The Philosopher's Club*
          Poems by Kim Addonizio
          Foreword by Gerald Stern